SUNDAY DRIVES

Michael Larson and Jill Larson Sundberg have collaborated on a number of books. These books include:

My Red Hat
My Red Hattitudes
Babes Remember
Cozy Cozy
Sunday Drives
There's Magic All Around Us

SUNDAY DRIVES

✦

Nostalgic Reminiscing with The Best of Burma-Shave

Michael Larson Jill Larson Sundberg

iUniverse, Inc.
New York Lincoln Shanghai

SUNDAY DRIVES
Nostalgic Reminiscing with The Best of Burma-Shave

iUniverse books may be ordered through booksellers or by contacting:

iUniverse
2021 Pine Lake Road, Suite 100
Lincoln, NE 68512
www.iuniverse.com
1-800-Authors (1-800-288-4677)

ISBN-13: 978-0-595-39324-4 (pbk)
ISBN-13: 978-0-595-67694-1 (cloth)
ISBN-13: 978-0-595-83720-5 (ebk)
ISBN-10: 0-595-39324-1 (pbk)
ISBN-10: 0-595-67694-4 (cloth)
ISBN-10: 0-595-83720-4 (ebk)

Printed in the United States of America

We dedicate this book to our parents,
Leonard Larson and Lois Larson, and to two
of our grandparents, Oscar Holte and Lottie Holte,
all of whom at one time or another put up with our antics during Sunday drives.

Introduction

Our love affair with Burma-Shave signs began a long time ago, during the 1950s, when father and mother would take us on Sunday drives. Often we took these trips to visit uncles and aunts and cousins, and it was easy to begin feeling bored in the car. Then, suddenly, some Burma-Shave signs would appear on the horizon, and the trip immediately would be fun again.

Burma-Shave signs date from the late 1920s. They first made their appearance in Southern Minnesota, where we grew up on a farm south of St. James.

Allan Odell, a wordsmith with the family that created Burma-Shave, came upon the idea for Burma-Shave signs when he saw a set of four signs along the side of a road broadcasting a gas station's oil and restrooms. Odell had been watching his father's company, the Burma-Vita Corp of Minneapolis, flirt with bankruptcy. Odell wondered if such signs might help stimulate sales for Burma-Shave, according to historian Bill Vossler, author of "Burma-Shave: The Rhymes, the Signs, the Times" (North Star Press, St. Cloud, Minn.).

With $200 worth of scrap lumber, Allan and his younger brother, Leonard, posted the first Burma-Shave signs along highways in Southern Minnesota. The Burma-Shave rhymes required five or six consecutive little signs just off the road so they could be read sequentially by motorists driving by.

Burma-Shave, the first brushless shaving cream in the United States, was sold from 1925 to 1966. It was the second brushless shaving cream ever to be manufactured, and it was the first one to become a success. Clinton Odell and his sons, Allan and Leonard, developed and sold the product. Together they formed the Burma-Vita company, named for a liniment, the company's first product. The Odells were losing their shirts on Burma-Vita and wanted to develop a product that people would use daily. A wholesale drug company in Minneapolis, where the company was based, told Clinton Odell about Lloyd's Euxesis. The British product was the first brushless shaving cream ever made, but it was a poor quality product. Clinton Odell hired a chemist named Carl Noren to develop a quality shaving cream. After 43 failed attempts, Noren finally created Burma-Shave.

The Burma-Shave craze expanded like shaving lather, and before the signs eventually disappeared, some 7,000 sets had popped up all across the United States and Canada. Burma-Shave signs appeared in every state except Arizona, Nevada and New Mexico. The company's creative people, supplemented by customers who sent in poems of their own, ultimately posted more than 600 different humorous jingles.

One favorite was, "Past schoolhouses/Please/Take it slow/
Let the little/Shavers grow. Burma-Shave," but there were plenty of other fun
ones:

"A peach/Looks good/With lots of fuzz/But man's no peach/And never was/
Burma-Shave"

"Don't take a curve/At 60 per/We hate to lose/
A customer/Burma-Shave"

"Does your husband/Misbehave/Grunt and grumble/
Rant and rave?/Shoot the brute/Some/Burma-Shave."

In 1963, the Burma-Vita Co. was sold to Phillip Morris Inc. Soon thereafter, the
remaining signs came down. The Phillip Morris company may have agreed with
poet Ogden Nash, who, in "Song of The Open Road," wrote, "I think that I shall
never see/A billboard lovely as a tree/Indeed, unless the billboards fall/I'll never
see a tree at all."

This book is intended to delight—to entertain those who remember the famous
Burma-Shave signs as well as those who want to learn what this craze was all
about. In the world of American advertising, Burma-Shave stood alone, develop-
ing a unique personality. The signs ultimately became part of the popular culture.
For many of us, recalling the clever advertising jingles helps us more fondly
remember those Sunday drives in the country—and the accompanying feelings of
safety and warmth and family. It's nostalgia that we're eager to help everyone
enjoy.

Michael Larson
Jill Larson Sundberg

We're widely read

And often quoted

But it's shaves

Not signs

For which we're noted

Burma-Shave

These signs

Are not

For laughs alone

The face they save

May be your own

Burma-Shave

A peach

Looks Good

With lots of fuzz

But man's no peach

And never was

Burma-Shave

Angels

Who guard you

While you drive

Usually retire at 65

Burma-Shave

Ben met Anna

Made a hit

She felt his chin

Ben-Anna split

Burma-Shave

The bearded lady

Tried a jar

Now she's a famous

Movie star

Burma-Shave

Cattle Crossing

Means Go Slow

That old bull

Is some cow's beau

Burma-Shave

Listen, birds

These signs cost

Money

So roost awhile

But don't get Funny.

Burma-Shave

Said farmer Brown

Who's bald

On top

Wish I could

Rotate the crop

Burma-Shave

Does your husband

Misbehave

Grunt and grumble

Rant and rave?

Shoot the brute

Some

Burma-Shave

Don't leave safety

To mere chance

That's why

Belts are

Sold with pants

Burma-Shave

He lit a match

To check his tank

That's why

They call him

Skinless frank

Burma-Shave

Slow down, Pa

Sakes alive

Ma missed

Signs

Four and five

Burma-Shave

The blackened forest

Smolders yet

Because

He flipped

A cigarette

Burma-Shave

Be a Noble

Not a Knave

Caesar Uses

Burma-Shave

Henry the Eighth

Sure had trouble

Short-term wives

Long-term stubble

Burma-Shave

She kissed the hairbrush

By mistake

She thought it was

Her husband Jake

Burma-Shave

The salesman

Taught the

Farmer's daughter

To plant

Her tu-lips

Where she oughter

Burma-Shave

Drinking drivers

Nothing worse

They put the quart

Before the hearse

Burma-Shave

The Midnight Ride

Of Paul for beer

Led to a warmer

Hemisphere

Burma-Shave

To steal

A kiss

He had the knack

But lacked the cheek

To get one back

Burma-Shave

Trains don't wander

All over the map

'Cause nobody sits

In the engineer's lap

Burma-Shave

She put

A bullet

Thru his hat

But he's had

Closer shaves than that

Burma-Shave

Feel your face

As you ride by

Now don't

You think

It's time to try?

Burma-Shave

Grandpa knows

It ain't too late

He's gone

To git

Some widder bait

Burma-Shave

The monkey took

One look at Jim

And threw the peanuts

Back at him

He needed

Burma-Shave

His tenor voice

She thought divine

'Til whiskers

Scratched

Sweet Adeline

Burma-Shave

Dinah doesn't

Treat him right

But if he'd

Shave

Dyna-mite!

Burma-Shave

Drove too long

Driver snoozing

What happened

Next is not amusing

Burma-Shave

To change that

Shaving job

To joy

You gotta use

The real McCoy

Burma-Shave

Toughest

Whiskers

In the town

We hold 'em up

You mow 'em down

Burma-Shave

His

Tomato

Was the mushy type

Until his beard

Grew over-ripe

Burma-Shave

Substitutes

Can do

More harm

Than city fellers

On a farm

Burma-Shave

The hobo

Lets his

Whiskers sprout

It's trains—not girls

That he takes out

Burma-Shave

Pedro

Walked

Back home by golly

His bristly chin

Was hot-to-Molly

Burma-Shave

Train approaching

Whistle squealing

Pause!

Avoid that

Rundown feeling!

Burma-Shave

Soap

May do

For lads with fuzz

But sir, you ain't

The kid you wuz

Burma-Shave

His cheek

Was rough

His chick vamoosed

And now she won't

Come home to roost

Burma-Shave

When Super-shaved

Remember, pard

You'll still get slapped

But not so hard

Burma-Shave

The whale

Put Jonah

Down the hatch

But coughed him up

Because he scratched

Burma-Shave

My job is

Keeping faces clean

And nobody knows

De stubble

I've seen

Burma-Shave

Her chariot

Raced at 80 per

They hauled away

What had

Ben Hur

Burma-Shave

Past schoolhouses

Please

Take it slow

Let the little

Shavers grow

Burma-Shave

Don't stick your elbow

Out too far

Or it may

Go home

In another car!

Burma-Shave

Don't lose your head

To save a minute

You need your head

Your brains are in it

Burma-Shave

Don't

Try passing

On a slope

Unless you have

A periscope

Burma-Shave

The wolf

Is shaved

So neat and trim

Red Riding Hood

Is chasing him

Burma-Shave

Don't take a curve

At 60 per

We hate to lose

A customer

Burma-Shave

This guy who drives

So close behind

Is he lonesome

Or just blind?

Burma-Shave

If your peach

Keeps out of reach

Better practice

What we Preach

Burma-Shave

Better try

Less speed per mile

That car

May have to

Last a while

Burma-Shave

A chin

Where barbed wire

Bristles stand

Is bound to be

A no-ma'ams land

Burma-Shave

She eyed

His beard

And said no dice

The wedding's off—

I'll COOK the rice

Burma-Shave

He had the ring

He had the flat

But she felt his chin

And that was that

Burma-Shave

Our fortune

Is your shaven face

It's our best

Advertising space

Burma-Shave

Brother speeder

Let's rehearse

All together

Good morning, Nurse

Burma-Shave

Around the curve

Lickety-split

Beautiful car

Wasn't it?

Burma-Shave

A guy who drives

A car wide open

Is not thinkin'

He's just hopin'

Burma-Shave

He's the guy

The girls forgot

Tho' he was smooth

His face was not

Burma-Shave

They missed the turn

The car went whizzin'

The fault was hern

The funeral hisn

Burma-Shave

Dim your lights

Behind a car

Let folks see

How bright you are

Burma-Shave

A beard

That's rough

And overgrown

Is better than

A chaperone

Burma-Shave

I know

He's a wolf

Said Riding Hood

But, Grandma, Dear

He smells so good

Burma-Shave

Spring

Has sprung

The grass has riz

Where last year's

Careless drivers is

Burma-Shave

Proper

Distance

To him was bunk

They pulled him out

Of some guy's trunk

Burma-Shave

If variety

Is what

You crave

Then get

A tuba

Burma-Shave

The band

For which

The grand stand roots

Is not made up

Of substi-toots!

Burma-Shave

Pat's bristles

Scratched

Bridget's nose

That's when

Her wild Irish rose

Burma-Shave

Missin' Kissin'?

Perhaps your thrush

Can't get thru

The underbrush—Try

Burma-Shave

At intersections

Look each way

A harp sounds nice

But it's hard to play

Burma-Shave

No matter the price

No matter how new

The best safety device

In the car is you

Burma-Shave

Unless

Your face

Is stinger free

You'd better let

Your honey be

Burma-Shave

Big blue tube

It's a honey

Best squeeze play

For love

Or money

Burma-Shave

My cheek

Says she

Feels smooth as satin

Ha! Ha! Says he

That's mine you're

Pattin'

Burma-Shave

When you lay

Those few cents down

You've bought

The smoothest

Shave in town

Burma-Shave

College boys,

Your courage muster

Shave off that fuzz

And cookie duster

Burma-Shave

We've made

Grandpa

Look so trim

The local

Draft board's after him

Burma-Shave

It gave

McDonald

That needed charm

Hello Hollywood

Good-by farm

Burma-Shave

Substitutes

Are like a girdle

They find some jobs

They just

Can't hurdle

Burma-Shave

If anything

Will please

Your Jill,

A little jack

For this jar will

Burma-Shave

The barefoot

Chap

With cheeks of tan

Won't let 'em chap

When he's a man

Burma-Shave

'No, no,'

She said

To her bristly beau

'I'd rather eat

The mistletoe.'

Burma-Shave

The bearded devil

Is forced

To dwell

In the only place

Where they don't sell

Burma-Shave

Why is it

When you

Try to pass

The guy in front

Goes twice as fast?

Burma-Shave

Substitutes

Can let you down

Quicker

Than a

Strapless gown

Burma-Shave

Burma-Shave

Was such a boom

They passed the bride

And kissed the groom

Burma-Shave

The place to pass

On curves

You know

Is only at

A beauty show

Burma-Shave

On curves ahead

Remember, sonny

That rabbit's foot

Failed

The bunny

Burma-Shave

To kiss

A mug

That's like a cactus

Takes more nerve

Than it does practice

Burma-Shave

Candidate says

Campaign

Confusing

Babies kiss me

Since I've been using

Burma-Shave

A Man A Miss

A Car A Curve

He kissed the Miss

And missed the Curve

Burma-Shave

Doesn't

Kiss you

Like she useter?

Perhaps she's seen

A smoother rooster!

Burma-Shave

Within this vale

Of toil

And sin

Your head grows bald

But not your chin

Burma-Shave

The draftee

Tried a tube

And purred

Well whaddya know

I've been defurred

Burma-Shave

Men

With whiskers

'Neath their noses

May need to kiss

Like eskimoses

Burma-Shave

Heaven's

Latest

Neophyte

Signaled left

Then turned right

Burma-Shave

We can't

Provide you

With a date

But we do supply

The best darn bait

Burma-Shave

Leaves

Face soft

As woman's touch

Yet doesn't cost you

Near as much

Burma-Shave

Car in ditch

Man in tree

Moon was full

So was he!

Burma-Shave

Use this cream

A day

Or two

Then don't call her—

She'll call you

Burma-Shave

At a quiz

Pa ain't

No whiz

But he knows how

To keep Ma his

Burma-Shave

If hugging

On highways

Is your sport

Trade in your car

For a Davenport

Burma-Shave

If Crusoe'd

Kept his chin

More tidy

He might have found

A lady Friday

Burma-Shave

The Big Blue Tub's

Just like Louise

You get a thrill

From every squeeze

Burma-Shave

These signs

We gladly

Dedicate

To men who've had

No date of late

Burma-Shave

Shaving brushes

You'll soon see 'em

On a shelf

In some museum

Burma-Shave

If you don't know

Whose signs these are

You haven't driven

Very far!

Burma-Shave

978-0-595-39324-4
0-595-39324-1

Made in the USA
San Bernardino, CA
14 February 2013